Famous Ghosts

By Michael Teitelbaum

The Child's World®
www.childsworld.com

Published in the United States of America by The Child's World®
P.O. Box 326 • Chanhassen, MN 55317-0326
800-599-READ • www.childsworld.com

ACKNOWLEDGMENTS

The Child's World®: Mary Berendes, Publishing Director

Produced by Shoreline Publishing Group LLC
President / Editorial Director: James Buckley, Jr.
Designer: Tom Carling, carlingdesign.com
Cover Art: Slimfilms
Copy Editor: Beth Adelman

Photo Credits
Interior—Corbis: 12; Getty Images: 19, 29; Clipart.com: 15, 17;
Dreamstime.com: 7, 8, 13, 21, 23; iStock: 5, 20, 24.

LIBRARY OF CONGRESS CATALOGING-IN-PUBLICATION DATA

Teitelbaum, Michael.
  Famous ghosts / by Michael Teitelbaum.
      p. cm. — (Boys rock!)
  Includes bibliographical references and index.
  ISBN 1-59296-729-9 (library bound : alk. paper)
 1. Ghosts—Juvenile literature. 2. Haunted places—Juvenile
literature. I. Title. II. Series.
  BF1461.T386 2006
  133.1—dc22
                              2006001633

CONTENTS

HAUNTED Places

A floorboard squeaks in the night. A door slams unexpectedly. Footsteps echo through an empty house. What's causing these strange noises?

There are perfectly normal answers for these kind of noises—mice, changes in temperature, or the wind. But some people think the answer lies in a world beyond ours—the world of ghosts.

What are ghosts? Some people believe ghosts are spirits of those who died unexpectedly. Some ghosts are looking to lend a helping hand, while others have **mischief** in mind. In this book you'll discover a wide variety of ghosts. So start reading, but leave a light on!

Not all ghosts are old. A theater in California that opened in the early 1990s already has a **resident** ghost.

Before the building was finished, some community leaders were given a tour. An older woman named Joan was on the tour. As she walked along an unfinished part of the stage, she lost her balance.

Sadly, Joan tumbled into a hole and fell 25 feet to the bottom of the construction site, where she died.

The theater was completed soon after, but strange things began happening. Theater workers started to wonder if Joan's spirit was still in the building. Had Joan become a a **poltergeist** (POHL-ter-guyst)?

Poltergeists like Joan haunt one place rather than moving around to different locations.

One night, a theater worker heard clanging footsteps high overhead. The sounds came from the metal **catwalks**—but the worker was the only person in the theater. Another person reported hearing noises coming from the sound system, even though it was turned off. Spotlights would suddenly flick on, even though no one was operating them. Almost everyone who has worked in the theater has reported feeling as if they were being watched. No one has ever been harmed by the poltergeist. It's thought that Joan's spirit just likes to let folks know she's still there.

Real or Not Real?

We're not saying that ghosts are real, or that they are imaginary. But all the stories in this book were reported by real people. We'll leave it up to you!

Is this New York home the most haunted house in America?

The most famous **haunted** house in the world just might be on Long Island, New York. A book and a movie, both called *The Amityville Horror,* were based on the story of this house.

The horrible haunting began in 1974, when six people living in the house were murdered there. The following year, the Lutz family moved into the house. Almost immediately, weird things began to happen. A heavy door blew down when there was no wind. Locked windows flew open by themselves, bending their thick metal frames.

One night, as the Lutz family gathered in the living room, a horrid-smelling slime

This is a poster for the very scary movie made about the haunted house in Amityville.

began dripping from the ceiling. Nothing upstairs was leaking. The disgusting slime came out of nowhere. Then the Lutzes noticed a pair of glowing red eyes peering in through the window. Outside, they found nothing—except a trail of hoofprints!

The final straw came in the middle of winter, when the house suddenly filled with flies.  The Lutz family had finally had enough. They left the house and never returned.

GHOSTLY
Children

Nothing is sadder than the death of a child. But is there anything scarier than the *ghost* of a child? In 1903, an Ohio **orphanage** burned down. Many children died in the fire.

To continue helping children in need, the orphanage was rebuilt on the same spot. The new building opened in 1906, and strange things started happening.

Children living there heard **wailing** and screaming coming from the hallway. Peeking out from their rooms, they saw ghostly children crying out for help!

The ghosts of the dead children haunted the place all the time. They were seen running down the stairs, screaming in fright, only to disappear before reaching the front door. Tiny handprints made of ash covered the walls.

One night, the children living in the orphanage woke up to the smell of smoke. Stepping from their rooms, they saw flames and smoke filling the hallway. As they ran to escape, the fire suddenly disappeared.

The new orphanage closed
just a few months later—
apparently due to the wishes
of the children who had died
in the 1903 fire. Ghosts, it
seems, just might be able to
make their voices heard in
the land of the living.

In another case of ghostly kids, a girl named Jennifer moved into a new house. She was thrilled to get her own room.

Bothered by a ghost in your house? Try this trick: put your shoes near the end of your bed, facing opposite ways. That is, point one toward the bed and one away from the bed. This supposedly upsets ghosts, and they leave!

The house itself was not really new. In fact, it was more than 100 years old. Many people had lived in the farmhouse. Some, as Jennifer found, never left.

One afternoon, while Jennifer was playing in her room, she looked up and saw a little girl standing in front of her. The girl was

dressed in old-fashioned
clothes—the kind people
wore in the 1800s.

"I'm Emily," the girl said.
"Will you play with me?"

Jennifer shut her eyes in disbelief. When she opened her eyes again, the little girl was gone. Soon, things started disappearing from Jennifer's room. First her favorite doll went missing, then her best hairbrush. She searched everywhere, but couldn't find them.

Ghost Money?

You might have ghosts in your pocket. Some U.S. paper money is printed in a special way to **foil** criminals who try to copy money. This type of printing is called *ghosting*. Hold a $20 bill up to the light and you'll see this "ghost" appear!

Then one day, her father was bringing some boxes up to the attic for storage. There he found the missing doll, the hairbrush, and other items. In the corner of the attic, he found an old, **yellowed** newspaper clipping. It described a girl named Emily who had died when she was just 8 years old. Emily had lived—and died—in that very house!

RESTLESS Spirits

Ghost stories tell of all kinds of sad events. One North Dakota ghost story is about a young woman with a young baby. The woman celebrated her wedding **anniversary** by putting on her white wedding dress and thinking back to her wedding day. Her anniversary should have been filled with happy memories—but it turned into a nightmare instead.

Going to check on her baby, the women discovered that he had died in his crib. The **grief-stricken** woman fled from her house, screaming as she ran down the road.

"Stricken" means hit hard or overcome by something.

23

She soon came to a bridge on a quiet country road. The woman stood on the bridge for hours, crying and staring at the swirling water. In her terrible sadness, she jumped off the bridge. She landed far below in the fast-running water, still wearing her dress.

Ever since then, some drivers who have crossed the bridge have reported hearing soft sobbing and wails of grief. Others have said they caught a peek of a woman in a white dress on the bridge.

Some reported feeling sad themselves. A few unlucky drivers have suddenly found a ghostly, crying woman dressed in white seated beside them in their cars!

Believe it or not, some people *want* to find ghosts! Ghost hunters use a variety of tools to try to track down—and shoo away—pesky ghosts.

Some ghosts seem to stay around to remember a special night. One evening in 1934, a 16-year-old girl named Mary went dancing with her boyfriend in Chicago.

The couple had a fight and Mary stormed out. She walked toward home along a dark, lonely stretch of road. As she walked, Mary was hit by a car and killed.

She was buried in a nearby cemetery in the dress and dancing shoes she was wearing that night.

Five years later, a young man named Jerry went to the same dance hall. There he met and danced with a beautiful young woman. He agreed to walk her home.

Sight, Sound, Smell, Touch

How do you know a ghost is around? People who claim to have experienced ghosts say they may appear as wisps of mist, balls of light, or even full human-like figures. They speak in soft voices. They create smells, and sometimes they even touch you!

On the way, Jerry gave her his jacket to help her keep warm on their walk.

When the couple reached the girl's house, she ran inside without saying a word. The next night, Jerry returned to the house to get his jacket. The parents who answered the door told him that their daughter, Mary, had died— five years earlier!

The parents showed Jerry a picture of Mary. It was the same girl he had walked home the night before.

He raced to the nearby
cemetery and found Mary's
grave—with his jacket
draped over the tombstone.

Are ghosts real or imagined?
No one knows for sure—but
we'd all love to find out!

GLOSSARY

anniversary a date people remember or celebrate because something happened on that date in the past

catwalks narrow walkways high above a theater stage, used by the workers

foil to stop someone from doing something

grief-stricken having terrible feelings of sadness or grief after a loss

haunted visited or lived in by a ghost

mischief an action that annoys or angers people, or that causes harm

orphanage a place where children who have no parents (orphans) may live

poltergeist a ghost that is responsible for unexplained noises or other mischief

resident living in a certain place for a while

wailing crying, moaning

yellowed the light yellow or tan color that newspapers turn as they get old and brittle

FIND OUT MORE

BOOKS

The Best Ghost Stories Ever
by Christopher Krovatin, Editor
(Scholastic, New York) 2004
Real-life stories of people who have seen ghosts and of places where ghosts have appeared.

Haunted Schools
by Allan Zullo
(Troll Communications, New York) 1996
Ghosts at school? Why not? This book tells the story of ghosts who live in schools around the world.

Horribly Haunted Houses
by Barbara Smith
(Ghost House Books, Edmonton, Alberta) 2005
Bring this book along if you're ever looking for a new house—these are the houses you *don't* want to live in!

WEB SITES

Visit our home page for lots of links about ghosts:
www.childsworld.com/links

Note to Parents, Teachers, and Librarians: We routinely check our Web links to make sure they're safe, active sites—so encourage your readers to check them out!

INDEX

MICHAEL TEITELBAUM has been a writer, editor, and producer of children's books, comic books, and magazines for more than 25 years. His recent nonfiction books include *Great Inventions: Radio & Television, Chinese Immigration*, and *Sports in America: The 1980s*. He also created and edited *Spider-Man Magazine*. Michael and his wife, Sheleigh, split their time between New York City and their 170-year-old farmhouse in upstate New York. They've never seen a ghost there!